Jim Crow On Trial: The Histo ... f the
S(

By Charles River Editors

A mob in Scottsboro in 1931

About Charles River Editors

Charles River Editors provides superior editing and original writing services across the digital publishing industry, with the expertise to create digital content for publishers across a vast range of subject matter. In addition to providing original digital content for third party publishers, we also republish civilization's greatest literary works, bringing them to new generations of readers via ebooks.

Sign up here to receive updates about free books as we publish them, and visit Our Kindle Author Page to browse today's free promotions and our most recently published Kindle titles.

Introduction

The Scottsboro Boys and defense counsel Samuel Leibowitz in 1932

The Scottsboro Boys

*Includes pictures

*Includes accounts of the case

*Includes online resources and a bibliography for further reading

*Includes a table of contents

"While the constitution guarantees to the accused a speedy trial, it is of greater importance that it should be by a fair and impartial jury, ex vi termini ('by definition'), a jury free from bias or prejudice, and, above all, from coercion and intimidation." – John C. Anderson, Chief Justice of the Alabama Supreme Court

"I'm interested solely in seeing that that poor…colored boy over there and his co-defendants in the other cases get a square shake of the dice, because I believe, before God, they are the victims of a dastardly frame up." – Samuel Leibowitz, defense attorney

When famous political philosopher Alexis de Tocqueville toured the new United States of America, he was impressed by the representative government set up by the Founders. At the same time, he ominously predicted, "If there ever are great revolutions there, they will be caused by the presence of the blacks upon American soil. That is to say, it will not be the equality of social conditions but rather their inequality which may give rise thereto." De Tocqueville was prescient, because the longest battle fought in the history of the United States has been the Civil Rights Movement. The framers of the Constitution kicked the problem down the road, over half a million died during the Civil War to end slavery, and then many more fought and died to dismantle segregation and legalized racism in the 100 years after.

It goes without saying that Jim Crow was pervasive in the wake of the Civil War, but few events in history put the effects of institutionalized segregation and racism on display like the case of the Scottsboro Boys, a group of black teenagers accused of raping two young white girls on a train. When the girls made the accusation, the teens were nearly lynched by an angry mob, only to be dragged almost immediately into court and given a sham trial that inevitably ended in a conviction by an all-white jury and death sentences for 8 of the 9 boys.

In the wake of the quick trial, the case was appealed by outsiders on behalf of the boys, and though Alabama's Supreme Court affirmed almost all the convictions, the attention raised nearly every potential issue implicating criminal procedure among the states. While the Bill of Rights had ensured a number of rights for criminal defendants, the states had previously been allowed to interpret those rights, leading to instances where defendants weren't provided adequate legal representation. The case of the Scottsboro Boys compelled the U.S. Supreme Court to order new trials in *Powell v. Arizona* (1932), which went a long way to determining and codifying some of the rights of criminal defendants in state courts.

However, even after one of the girls recanted her testimony during retrials, the Scottsboro Boys were still found guilty, leading to more appeals and yet another Supreme Court ruling ordering retrials. Eventually, some of the boys were cleared of charges, but several still ended up serving time in prison, and it would not be until 80 years after the controversial case that Alabama posthumously pardoned the defendants who hadn't been cleared of all charges. To this day, the case remains synonymous with the injustice of Jim Crow and the manner in which African Americans were deprived of basic civil rights, and historian Wayne Flynt may have put it best when he summed up the case and its aftermath: "I think that's perhaps an ultimate tragedy. People pulled into history who never wanted to be pulled into history suddenly put on a national platform, and tragically paraded out for everybody's benefit but their own. And the question of who really cared about them, who really defended them? Almost everyone had an agenda that involved the Scottsboro Boys. And I think the courage of the Scottsboro Boys is just surviving, just enduring."

Jim Crow On Trial: The History and Legacy of the Notorious Case of the Scottsboro Boys chronicles the infamous crime and the notorious trial that followed. Along with pictures of important people, places, and events, you will learn about one of the most controversial cases in American history like never before.

Jim Crow On Trial: The History and Legacy of the Notorious Case of the Scottsboro Boys

About Charles River Editors

Introduction

Chapter 1: No Novel Thing to Meet New People

"While sitting down worried nearly crazy I want you all to write to me and tell me how is things going on about this case of us 9 boys because I am in here for something I know I did not do. My pour [sic] mother has no one to help her to make a living but me. She had a little girl...only 5 years old to take [care] of and she has no job at all and I just.... You all know how times is on the outside times I had I did all I could for my pour [sic] mother to help her live and my little sister. I was on my way to Memphis on an oil tank by myself alone and I was not worried with anyone until I got to Paint Rock, Alabama and they just made a frame up on us boys just cause they could. ... We want you all to send us some money so we can buy us something that we can eat, this food don't agree with me at all. I [am] supposed to be at home anyway. I did not do what they got me for. I ain't give no one any cause to mistreat me this way. I know I ain't and I hope you all is doing all you can for us boys." - Letter from Olen Montgomery to George Chamlee, May 25, 1931

When the Southern Rail Corporation engine left Chattanooga, Tennessee on the morning of March 25, 1931, those driving it likely knew that there were hobos on board. In the early days of what would come to be known as the Great Depression, thousands of out-of-work men and women regularly "rode the rails" across the country in empty boxcars, looking for work, and through it, hope.

Of course, the tensions of the times, brought on by such desperate circumstances, also ensured that problems often broke out on the trains, and this day was no different. During the trip, a white man stepped on the hands of Haywood Patterson, one of nine African American teenagers riding atop the box car. Patterson later complained, "We was just mindin' our own business, when one of them said, 'This is a white man's train. All you N***** bastards unload.' But we weren't goin' nowhere so there was a fight. We got the best of it and threw them off."

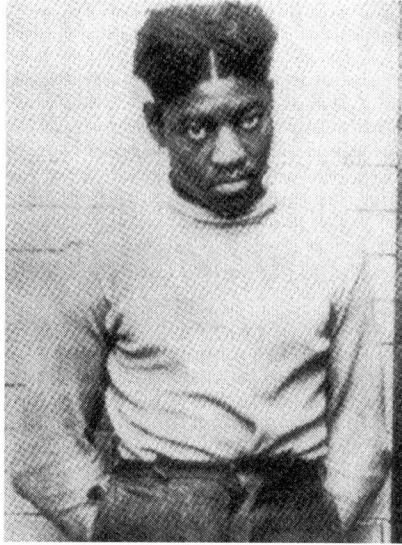

Patterson

By the time the train reached its next stop, the conductor had called ahead and told those in charge there had been a fight on the train, so a group of men from Paint Rock, Alabama approached the train when it stopped and began searching for the black men they assumed caused the problem. As it turned out, they found much more than they bargained for, because while the men were looking around, two women, clad in masculine overalls and looking traumatized, emerged from around the side of one of the boxcars. Their names were Ruby Bates and Victoria Price, and they were about to make their way into the history books, beginning when one of them cried out, "We've been raped. All those colored boys raped us."

Ruby Bates and Victoria Price

These were the most terrifying words a black man living in 1930s America could hear, especially in rural Alabama. Roy Wright, then only 13 years old, remembered, "The firstest I knowed anything was wrong, or knowed who else was on that train was when that crowd of white men stopped the train and Paint Rock and took us off. They took us up the railroad bank to a white rock and stood us against it with their guns aimed at our heads. One of the white men said to me, 'Come on now, n*****, tell us who pushed those white boys off the train, 'cause we don't want to punish anybody but the guilty ones. If you tell us which ones did it we'll let you others go.' And I told them I didn't know anything about it and hadn't seen nothing. Then one of them said to me, 'You know, n*****, we don't let no darkies hang around here, and if we catch you anywhere near here after dark we'll shoot you. Now get going.' Andy (that's my brother), Haywood, Eugene and me -- we started away. Nobody said nothing until we had walked some little way and then they called us back and loaded us on a truck, tied our hands and feet with rope and carried us to the jail in Scottsboro..."

Roy Wright

19 year old Clarence Norris described the hectic scene in the wake of the girls' claims: "The place was surrounded with a mob. They had shotguns, pistols, sticks, pieces a' iron, everything. The crowd commenced to hollerin' let's take these black son-or-a-bitches up here and put 'em to a tree. I just thought that I was gonna die. … Cars, trucks, they was comin' in all kinds of ways, the mob was. 'Bring them n****** outta there. If you don't bring them out, we'll come in and get 'em.' That's all you could hear, all over that little town."

Norris

Frank Grigg, one of the white men there that day, recalled, "Mr. Broadway sent up to the store to get a skein, I never did hear that word before, a skein of plough line, and the rope was cut into pieces where they could tie the hands of the ones that was under arrest. And the next thing was, how we going to get them to Scottsboro?"

As the accounts suggest, it had been quickly decided that the thing to do was to load the nine boys onto the back of a pickup truck and take them to Scottsboro, the nearest town that had a jail in which to house them. The group of boys included Patterson (18), Norris (19), Roy Wright (12 or 13), his brother Andy Wright (19), Charlie Weems (16), Eugene Williams (13), Willie Roberson (16), Ozie Powell (16) and Olen Montgomery (17), all of whom were jailed that day.

Montgomery

Powell

Roberson

Williams

Andy Wright

As the group arrived in the community, many people stopped what they were doing to point and stare, and among those stunned by the sight of nine black teenagers tied up in the back of a truck driven by a white man and followed by others were Jackson County Sheriff Matt L. Wann's sons. Billie Wann explained, "Crowds were beginning to form outside the jail.....The rumor was that they were going to go into the jail. There was already poles outside that they were going to break the door down with." However, once the men were delivered to Sheriff Wann, he made it clear that there would be no lynching on his watch. His son Robert later recalled, "On March 25, 1931, a friend and I were playing basketball on the side of the Jackson County jail. And we noticed a flatbed stake-body truck stop in front of the jail with a guard with rifles on each corner. They quickly unloaded the prisoners. … As the situation became desperate, my father took his pistol off and he gave it to his deputies.... he walked out the front door right through the middle of the mob and the crowd separated for him, not a hand touched him. He went to the courthouse and called the governor."

A portrait of Sheriff Wann

That same day, *The New York Times* reported on the incident: "Fearing a mob outbreak at Scottsboro, county seat of Jackson County, following the arrest of nine Negroes charged with attacking two white girls, a detachment of militia was ordered to the Jackson County jail tonight. Sheriff Wann at Scottsboro asked for troops when a crowd which had gathered about the jail became threatening. The Sheriff wired to Montgomery that the crowd numbered 300. Later, however, the sheriff reported that the mob was dispersing as the night was cold, and danger seemed averted. The girls, who gave their names as Ruby Bates, 23, and Victoria Price, 18, were in a box car with seven white men when the Negro tramps got in at a point between Stevenson and Scottsboro. They threw six of the white men off the train. The seventh and the girls are said to have fought desperately until the white man was knocked unconscious. The men who had been thrown out of the car telegraphed ahead to Paint Rock. When the train arrived there a Sheriff's posse surrounded the car and captured the Negroes after a short fight. The Negro prisoners and their white accusers were taken to Scottsboro where the Negroes were formally charged with criminal assault on a woman, a capital offense in Alabama. The white men who had been in the box car were held as material witnesses."

Over the next several weeks, Victoria Price became the spokesperson for both women, and she described the alleged rape in vivid detail: "I was riding on a freight train that was traveling through Jackson County, Alabama, to Paint Rock, Alabama. I was on that train when it reached Stevenson. Ruby Bates was riding with me on that train. After the train left Stevenson, Alabama, coming this way in the direction of Paint Rock, I was riding in a gondola car. Ruby Bates and several white boys were in the car with me. The car had chert in it, what I heard called chert. It laced about a foot and half or 3 feet of being full. ... All these twelve men jumped into the gondola over mine and Ruby Bates' head. ... Some one of them, I don't know which one it was, he said, 'All You white sons of bitches unload.' Two of them had pistols to the best of my recollection. ... Some of them had knives in their hands as they got into the gondola car. I wouldn't say, but to the best of my knowledge some of them had them open. After one of them said, 'All you white sons of bitches unload,' the following then happened on that car, between this man or anybody else: they knocked them off and begun to run up and down the side to see that they did not get back on, i.e., the white boys they had knocked off, except Gilley. Then they commenced to attack us girls, me and Ruby Bates. They put their hands on me. After they got the white boys off, I went to the corner of the gondola to get over, and one of the crowd in the back of the car, 'We are not going to hurt you,' and when I started to make my jump he hit me, he hit me, and one of them pulled off my clothes, my overalls-They taken my overalls off and then they taken me and threw me over on the chert, and one of them held my legs, and one held a knife on me there, and then one of them raped me and Ruby Bates."

Chapter 2: While In My Cell

"While in my cell, lonely and thinking of you. I am trying by some means to write you a few words. I would like for you to come down here Thursday. I feel like I can eat some of your cooking Mom. Beatrice made like she was going to send me a chicken but I haven't got one yet. I would like for you to bring or send me a chicken. If you please, send me some paper and stamps so I can write more often. Be sure to send me that chicken, if nothing else and don't forget that. Please don't write or tell me anything to make me feel good. You can't send Andy anything to eat, but you can me. Send or bring me a big bag of peanuts. If you send me a box you don't have to come because I have your picture and I can look at it. Or the cake slice it up when you send it. Tell Sis I say hello. Write back. Let me know if you send it or come down. Either one. Put in box or let it come on to me. I have gone chicken crazy so I close for this time." - Letter from Roy Wright to his mother, June 19, 1931

The state authorities wasted no time in prosecuting the accused; court convened on Monday, April 6, 1931, the first "court day" available. Perhaps not surprisingly, this day brought more than the usual influx of hundreds into the city, as thousands came to town for the big trial. Frank Grigg, who had been on the scene when the boys were being taken to Jonesboro, was also there for the trial: "I saw many strangers, lots of strangers. I saw a carload over here and a carload over there. I saw Tennessee tags and Georgia tags. And some of them were armed, most of them had shotguns." Archie Stewart, a Scottsboro resident, noted the efforts taken to assure a lynch mob couldn't get the defendants: "They had strings up so the mob could not get up beyond the string.

So whenever the guard would pass, the crowd would push beyond the sting, and the guard would turn on his heels, throw his gun down, and say:' get back!' But as soon as he would turn his back, they were back again."

The men were tried in four separate trials, with Norris and Weems, the oldest two, going first. According to Hollace Ransdall, who was writing for the American Civil Liberties Union (ACLU), "The chief witness for the State was the older of the two girls, Victoria Price, who told the story of the trip to Chattanooga and back from Huntsville, as given previously. She did it with such gusto, snap and wise-cracks, that the courtroom was often in a roar of laughter. Her flip retorts to the attorney for the defense, Steven Roddy, especially caused amusement. The sentiment of the courtroom was with her, she knew it and played up to it, as can be seen by the record of the trial testimony. The other girl, Ruby Bates, was found by the prosecution to be a 'weak witness,' as I was told several times by officials present at the trial. The white youth, Orvil Gilley, who remained on the train with the girls, also was considered stupid and slow-witted. The Gilley boy came from Albertville, a small village a short distance from Scottsboro. Judge Hawkins remarked to me about him, saying, 'Well, we all know what his family is. Her mother, for instance . . .' and he broke off as if it were too obvious for words what his mother was like. I asked if he meant that the family was feeble minded or of low mentality. 'No, not that,' he replied, 'but . . . well we know here they are not much good.' He would commit himself no farther."

Weems

According to Ransdall, the medical experts and the prosecution's other witnesses were not much more convincing than the young women were. Ransdall continued, "Dr. M. H. Lynch, County Health Physician, and Dr. H. H. Bridges, of Scottsboro, testified at the trial that the medical examination of the girls made shortly after they were taken from the train, showed that both the girls had had recent sexual intercourse, but that there were no lacerations, tears, or other signs of rough handling; that they were not hysterical when brought to the doctor's office first, but became so later. Dr. Bridges said that Victoria had a small scratch on her neck and a small bruise or two, but nothing more serious was found. The lawyer for the defense, Mr. Roddy, inquired hesitantly and indirectly, in his cross-examination of the doctor, if it were possible to tell the difference between the spermatozoa of a white man and that of a colored male. The doctor answered that it was not possible to distinguish any difference. Other witnesses put on the stand by the State included Luther Morris, a farmer living west of Stevenson, who testified that he had seen the girls and the Negroes on the freight train as it passed his hay loft, which he said was 30 miles away, and that he 'had seen a plenty;' Lee Adams, of Stevenson, who said he saw the fight between the white and colored boys on the train, and Charles Latham, deputy who captured the Negroes at Paint Rock."

Unfortunately, the defense was unable to take the best advantage of the prosecution's weak case, in large measure due to the fact the men were represented by a real estate attorney that their parents quickly had to hire for $60. Ransdall reported, "Mr. Steven Roddy, attorney for the defense from Chattanooga, was undoubtedly intimidated by the position in which he found himself. At the beginning of the trial he had asked not to be recorded as the lawyer in the case, begging the judge to leave Milo Moody, Scottsboro attorney appointed by the Judge as lawyer for the defense, on record as counsel for the Negroes with himself appearing purely in advisory capacity as representing the parents and friends of the boys in Chattanooga. He made little more than half-hearted attempts to use the formalities of the law to which he was entitled, after his motion for a change of venue made at the beginning of the trial was overruled. It might be said for him, of course, that taking the situation as it was, he felt it was hopeless for him to attempt to do anything much, except make motions for a new trial after the convictions, which he did."

The first two men were convicted and sentenced on Tuesday afternoon, and the next day, Patterson was convicted after being the only man tried alone. Five others - Montgomery, Wright, Williams, Robeson and Powell - were also convicted in short order, and all eight of the men had been sentenced to death. As the prosecutor had put it during closing arguments against Norris and Weems, "If you don't give these men death sentences, the electric chair might as well be abolished."

Finally, it was 13 year old Wright's turn, and he later described his harrowing experience: "I was sitting in a chair in front of the judge and one of those girls was testifying. One of the deputy sheriffs leaned over to me and asked me if I was going to turn State's evidence, and I said no, because I didn't know anything about this case. Then the trial stopped awhile and the deputy sheriff beckoned to me to come out into another room -- the room back of the place the judge was sitting -- and I went. They whipped me and it seemed like they was going to kill me. All the time they kept saying, 'Now will you tell?' and finally it seemed like I couldn't stand no more and I said yes. Then I went back into the courtroom and they put me up on the chair in front of the judge and began asking a lot of questions, and I said I had seen Charlie Weems and Clarence Norris in the gondola car with the white girls." When he was no longer under duress, Wright later recanted his testimony and admitted, "I didn't see no white girls and no white boys either."

As it turned out, Wright's cooperation did him no favors, as Ransdall explained the result in his case: "Several of the authorities at the trial assured me that he was really the worst of the lot and deserved no lenience on account of his youth. But for the sake of outside public opinion, the State decided to ask for life imprisonment instead of the death penalty, in view of the youth of the defendant. At two o'clock on the afternoon of Thursday, April 9, the jury announced that they were dead-locked and could not agree on a verdict. Eleven of them stood for the death penalty and one for life imprisonment. Judge Hawkins declared a mistrial, and the child was ordered back to jail to await another ordeal at a later date. He is now in the Birmingham jail."

The eight older boys who were convicted were to be taken to Kilby Prison, located just outside Montgomery, Alabama, and that evening, the convicted men staged a riot to protest their innocence. On April 11, the *Associated Press* reported, "Protesting against their sentences, eight negroes condemned to death at Scottsboro yesterday for attacking two white girls rioted in the Etowah County jail today, but were subdued by guards, who placed them in irons. The Negroes, who were returned here under military escort after being sentenced for attacking the girls traveling as hoboes, aboard a freight train, shouted demands for special food, beat on the cell bars and tore up the bedding. Their shouts were heard some distance from the jail and Sheriff T. L. Griffin, who occupies an apartment on the lower floor of the jail, removed his family. Sheriff Griffin appealed to military authorities for aid, and colonel W. M Thompson and Captain C.C. Whitehead went to the jail. With sufficient guards to prevent an attempted break, the 'Bull pen,' in which the Negroes were confined, was opened and guards handcuffed the prisoners in pairs. Governor Miller at Montgomery today received protests in the case from the International Labor Defense in New York and the League of Struggle for Negro Rights of New York and the Anti-Imperialist League of the United States. All charged the Negroes 'were railroaded.' The governor declined to comment."

Kilby Prison

The boys soon learned that their actions were putting their lives in imminent danger. Patterson explained, "The cell door banged open. They beat on us with their fists, they kicked and tramped on our legs. The sheriff said to me: 'see that gallows, n*****. If you don't quieten' down I'll take you around to that gallows and hang you myself.'"

Chapter 3: Fighting for Us Boys

"While sitting all alone in prison I thought I'll express you a few lines to let you here from us boys. We are all well and hoping to be free soon and also hoping you all will remain in fighting for us boys. Mr. Engdahl I am ask you a question and I would like for you to answer it in your writing, and here it's are. Have you all got Mr. Darrow fighting for us boys? The reasons why I ask you that because I heard that Mr. Clarence Darrow was going to fighting for us boys, and I would like to know if possible because I am innocent, as innocent as the tiny mite of life just beginning to stir beneath my heart. Honest, Mr. Engdahl, I haven't did anything to be imprisonment like this. And all of the boys send their best regards to you all and best wishes. So I would appreciate an interview at your earliest convenience." - Letter from Haywood Patterson to Mr. J. Louis Engdahl, December 10, 1931

In the wake of their death sentences, the boys and the story may all have come to an end if the

Communist Party of the United States had not stepped in. At the time, this organization was seen by many to be the only hope for equal rights for black workers. According to former Communist Party member Lloyd Brown, "The view was that in the South we had an uncompleted revolution. The abolition of slavery had not been really fulfilled [since] we now had sharecropping. We had literally tens of thousands of people who were bound to the farm in debt, work all year, at the end of the year they would have nothing left. We felt that the system was maintained only in one way: by terror. Terror -- if you get out of line you're lynched."

At the same time, the Communists had not counted on how ingrained the roles of blacks and whites was in the Southern psyche. Determined to stir up controversy, the Party seized on the Scottsboro incident to draw attention to the plight of blacks in the South, and even Brown admitted, "We were propagandizing. There's just no doubt, we were using, yes. We were using the Scottsboro case to expose what was going on in the South."

Within a few weeks, the Communists had organized the first of many demonstrations on behalf of the men. The *New York Times* reported, "Two hundred communists undertook to march down Lenox Avenue through the center of Harlem yesterday afternoon in defiance of the police. Fifteen minutes later, when twenty policemen had replaced their nightsticks and the screams of women in the crowd had died down, the sidewalk was strewn with communist banners." The party also sent lawyers south to the prison to visit the men in Kilby and convince them to let them appeal their cases. However, the men themselves did not know how to handle the important white lawyers and the communist committee ended up going through their parents to get their permission to move forward. Mary Licht, one of the organizers involved, later said, "I told them if the International Labor Defense comes we don't believe in just having a trial. We believe in masses of people being behind the causes you're fighting for, and that's how the International Labor Defense Works."

Once the Communists had publicized the case, they spread the word of "American injustice" around the world, and suddenly the United States government found itself hearing about protests against it racial policies in such far off places as Germany and Russia. On July 1, the *Times* reported, "Communist newspapers, to which may be attributed responsibility for recent mob attacks on the American Consulates at Dresden and Leipzig, are making a capital of the Scottsboro convictions. They are fervently appealing to Reds everywhere to 'save the victims of judicial murder,' asserting that the Negroes are wholly innocent of the crimes for which they were sentenced. A gang of young Communists smashed half a dozen windows of the American Consulate General in Bellevue Street late tonight. Police captured five. Following communistic rioting in the East Side, in which one policeman was shot dead, Berlin's Chief of Police banned the huge International Communist Athletic Meet scheduled for next Sunday."

As the case got more attention, the National Association for the Advancement of Colored People (NAACP) also wanted to make the most of the plight of the "Scottsboro Boys."

Moreover, they were (justifiably) concerned that the involvement of communists might hinder rather than help their case. However, when African American leaders attempted to conduct their own protest in Camp Hill, Alabama, things ended badly, as the *Associated Press* told readers on July 18, 1931: "A meeting of Negro radicals near here last night at which Governor B.M. Miller was threatened with violence unless he liberated the eight Negroes sentenced to death for attacking two white girls led to clashes with posses today in which on Negro was killed, two white officers and three Negroes were wounded and seventeen Negroes were arrested. An armed posse was summoned late today from Tallapoosa and Lee Counties as reports spread that Negro radicals planned a second protest meeting tonight in the woods near Waverly, Ala. A small house occupied by a Negro family near the place where the meeting was held was destroyed by fire soon afterward. … A posse of eight men, reported from Notasulga, Ala., late today that they were still trailing a Negro from Chattanooga, Tenn., who for two months has been organizing Negroes in this section in what confiscated minute books described as "the Society for the Advancement of Colored People." Chief of Police J.M. Wilson said that last night's meeting was in protest against the death sentence imposed against the eight Negroes at Scottsboro, Ala., in April."

Governor Miller

Then, the NAACP announced that it had secured America's most prominent attorney to defend the boys. *The New York Times* reported on December 28, 1931, "Clarence Darrow and Arthur Garfield Hays of New York were here today preparing to take the defense of the eight Negroes convicted and sentenced to death at Scottsboro on a charge of attacking two white girls on March 25. Mr. Darrow said that he and Mr. Hays had been retained by the National Association for the Advancement of Colored People. They will spend a day or two in Birmingham consulting local lawyers connected with the trial and then will return to New York. The Supreme Court has set Jan. 18 as the date for hearing the motion for a new trial, and Mr. Darrow and Mr. Hays will appear before the court then. If a new trial is granted they will be in charge of the defense. Among the other agencies that have interested themselves in the Negroes is the International Labor Defense League, which has retained George Chamblee of Chattanooga, former Attorney General of Tennessee. During the last nine months Governor Miller has received protests on their sentences from England, Germany, France, Switzerland, Canada, Cuba, several South American countries and many places in this country."

Darrow

By the 1930s, Clarence Darrow was considered the best criminal defense attorney in the country, and he was best known for defending Leopold and Loeb, two young adults who had murdered a teenager in hopes of committing the perfect crime. His work on that case helped lead to his participation in the Scopes Monkey Trial, where he went head to head against William Jennings Bryan. Darrow had grown up in Kinsman, Ohio, and he was known as a rapid reader and the town atheist. He was also the progressive's progressive, once opining that society "is nothing less than organized injustice."

Despite the protests, or perhaps in part due to them, the Scottsboro Boys sat in prison for nearly a year while the NAACP gave speeches, the communists protested, and Alabama's Supreme Court affirmed the convictions on appeal. The Alabama Supreme Court ruled 7-2 in favor of upholding the verdicts, but Alabama's Chief Justice, John C. Anderson, took issue with the proceedings in the lower court and made passionate arguments in his dissent. Speaking of Steven Roddy's work as defense counsel, Anderson noted Roddy "declined to appear as appointed counsel and did so only as amicus curiae." Anderson also pointed out how the system had impeded the defendants' rights: "These defendants were confined in jail in another county...and local counsel had little opportunity to...prepare their defense...[they] would have been represented by able counsel had a better opportunity been given." Anderson also took issue with the fact the defense hadn't even bothered to give a closing argument, further proof that Roddy was literally just going through the motions. The Chief Justice concluded, "No matter how revolting the accusation, how clear the proof, or how degraded or even brutal, the offender, the Constitution, the law, the very genius of Anglo-American liberty demand a fair and impartial trial."

In November 1932, the Communists staged a large-scale protest in Washington, D.C., and though they were eventually run off by police, their lawyers, speaking inside before the U.S. Supreme Court, were heard. The Court's 7-2 ruling in *Powell v. Alabama* (1932) ended up being a seminal one for assuring that criminal defendants were given due process in state courts, and the Court reversed the convictions because the boys had not had an adequate defense, requiring Alabama to schedule new trials. The Supreme Court's holding that the 14th Amendment required state trials to comply with the 6th Amendment's guarantee of adequate counsel for defendants would help lead to a system in which public defenders were provided to indigent defendants.

Writing for the majority, Justice George Sutherland explained, "In the light of the ... ignorance and illiteracy of the defendants, their youth, the circumstances of public hostility, the imprisonment and the close surveillance of the defendants by the military forces, the fact that their friends and families were all in other states and communication with them necessarily difficult, and above all that they stood in deadly peril of their lives—we think the failure of the trial court to give them reasonable time and opportunity to secure counsel was a clear denial of due process. But passing that, and assuming their inability, even if opportunity had been given, to employ counsel, ... under the circumstances just stated, the necessity of counsel was so vital and imperative that the failure of the trial court to make an effective appointment of counsel was likewise a denial of due process within the meaning of the Fourteenth Amendment."

At the same time, Sutherland explicitly wrote that the Court intended to limit the ruling only to cases involving the death penalty: "Whether this would be so in other criminal prosecutions, or under other circumstances, we need not determine. All that it is necessary now to decide, as we do decide, is that in a capital case, where the defendant is unable to employ counsel, and is incapable adequately of making his own defense because of ignorance, feeble-mindedness, illiteracy, or the like, it is the duty of the court, whether requested or not, to assign counsel for him as a necessary requisite of due process of law; and that duty is not discharged by an assignment at such a time or under such circumstances as to preclude the giving of effective aid in the preparation and trial of the case. ... In a case such as this, whatever may be the rule in other cases, the right to have counsel appointed, when necessary, is a logical corollary from the constitutional right to be heard by counsel." Decades later, the Court's ruling in *Gideon v.*

Wainwright extended the ruling in *Powell* to non-capital cases.

Sutherland

Chapter 4: Made Me Tell a Lie

"I want to make a statement too you: Mary Sanders is a goddam lier [sic] about those Negroes jazzing me. Those policemen made me tell a lie. That is my statement because I want too clear myself, that is all to it. If you want too [sic] believe, ok. If not that is ok. You will be sorry someday if you had to stay in jail with eights Negroes. You would tell a lie, too. Those Negroes did not touch me or those white boys. I hope you will believe me, the law don't. I love you better than Mary does or anybody else in the world. That is why I am telling you of this thing. I was drunk at the time and did not know what I was doing. I know it was wrong to let those Negroes die on account of me. I hope you will believe my statement because it is the God's truth. I hope you will believe me. I was jazzed but those white boys jazzed me. I wish those Negroes are not burnt on account of me. It is these white boys' fault. That is my statement and that is all I know. I hope you tell the law; hope you will answer. P.S. This is one time that I might tell a lie but it is the truth so God help me." - Letter from Ruby Bates to Earl Streetman, January 5, 1932

The Communists' legal team had won at the highest court in the land, but the boys were hardly out of the woods with a retrial on the horizon. Their counsel would still have to try to prove the boys were not guilty of the charges against them. The NAACP had already hired Clarence Darrow, so the Communists went to Samuel Leibowitz, a Darrow rival who had had never lost any of the 78 murder cases he had worked. A fabulous researcher, he was also known for his ability to sway and charm a jury.

Leibowitz

At first, Leibowitz did not want to get mixed up with the Communist movement, but his ambition finally got the best of him and he could not resist the chance to work on one of the most controversial cases of the century. Thus, he agreed to take the case, and the Party's legal organization, the International Labor Defense (ILD), persuaded the boys to reject Darrow and accept him as their lead attorney. With that, the stage was set for one of the most controversial trials in American history.

The retrial began in Decatur, Alabama in April 1933 thanks to a successful change of venue, and hundreds of people crowded into the courthouse and outside on the grounds anxious to see and hear what the Yankee attorney was going to do. Athlene Banks was there that day and later said, "I went because of history. I had never seen anything like that before, and I wanted to know just how it would be carried on. When we entered the courtroom, we were not told the way to go, we knew the way to go: because it was black on one side and white on the other."

Even before the trial began, Leibowitz was aware of the problems being caused by some of the Northern "instigators" who had come South in the hopes of stirring up trouble. On April 3, 1933, the *New York Times* reported that "visitors from New York had left town along with several others who came here in the capacity of 'observer' in the trial of a case which the International Labor Defense and its Communist affiliates have been used as propaganda for organization work among the Negroes. It was understood that the exodus was ordered by Mr. Leibowitz as a condition of his continuing as trial counsel. Explaining his attitude, Mr. Leibowitz said: 'I am not interested in the affairs of the Republican party, the Democratic party, the Socialist party, the Communist party or any other group in the conduct of this case. I am interested solely in saving these innocent boys from the electric chair, and I will do my best to see that their case is not endangered by propaganda or agitation from any quarter. I have ordered the irresponsibles away and they must stay away.'"

One of Leibowitz's first moves was to convince the court to try each man separately. Thus, Haywood Patterson stood alone before the judge on the first morning of the first trial. He was chosen by the prosecutor, Attorney General Thomas Knight, because he was already notorious for his bad behavior. Van Glasscock, who was with the National Guard at the time, once commented, "Patterson was mean. I looked him in the eye first time we brought him out of jail. I saw he'd kill if he got a chance."

Knight

Judge James Horton, who Leibowitz's son Robert later described as "a Lincolnesque-type thorough Southern gentleman," presided over the case, and under his watchful gaze, the two lawyers seated a jury of 12 white men. Of course, this was not on account of an oversight by Leibowitz; the simple fact was that by disenfranchising black people, Alabama made it virtually impossible for a black person to be a juror.

Horton

However, when it came time for the trial to begin, one of the prosecution's star witnesses, Ruby Bates, was missing. Thus, it was Victoria Price's lurid testimony that the jury heard first: "I hollered for help until they stopped me, until some of them knocked me in the head with the butt-end of a gun. They unfastened my overalls while I was standing up and then they threw me down on the gravel and finished pulling them off my feet. This Negro grabbed me by the legs and pulled them open and then one of them put a knife on my throat, and one got on top of me."

Price had never had her story seriously challenged until Leibowitz finally got his chance to cross-examine her. At the same time, the famed lawyer was about to meet a truly uncooperative and hostile witness. Price's caustic wit was entirely on display during this exchange:

> "Leibowitz: Just look at this little replica and tell me it fairly represents the general appearance of the box car you rode on?

> "Price: It kinda represents one, but it ain't like the one I was on.

> "Leibowitz: In what way is it different, can you say?

> "Price: I won't say.

"Leibowitz: If you can't say, why do you say it is different?

"Price: Because that is not the train I was on. It was bigger, lots bigger -- that is a toy."

No matter how he came at her, Price stuck to her story, saying again and again when challenged, "I can't remember." For Leibowitz, it was like questioning a brick wall, but some of those in the audience at least saw a problem with what she was saying. Athlene Banks observed, "I feel if you are telling the truth you could look anybody in the eye. Victoria never looked directly. It was almost to the floor. Until she was made angry, and then she would shout, 'I don't know anything. I told you that before, and I'll tell it to you again.'"

A picture of Price testifying

Another problem lay in Price's claim that she had spent the night prior to her attack at a boarding house in Chattanooga. She said a Mrs. Callie Brochie owned the house, but Leibowitz insisted no such woman or place existed.

"Leibowitz: You went to bed in the lady's house?

"Price: Yes sir.

"Leibowitz: Was it one floor or two floor?

"Price: I don't remember, four or five room house.

"Leibowitz: What sort of food, what did you do in the evening, what sort of bed or room?

"Price: I don't know.

"Leibowitz: By the way, Mrs. Price, as a matter of fact the name of Mrs. Callie you apply to this boarding house lady is the name of a boarding house lady used in the Saturday Evening Post stories: isn't that where you got the name?

"Price: I ain't never heard of that Callie!

"Leibowitz: The truth about Callie Brochie was that she was a fictional character in stories that appeared in the Saturday Evening Post. There was no Callie Brochie on Seventh Street in Chattanooga."

…

"Leibowitz: Did you tell a man by the name of Lester Carter that you would introduce him to Ruby?

"Price: I told you, I never seen Lester Carter before.

"Leibowitz: Isn't it a fact that the night before you left Chattanooga you and your boyfriend and Ruby and Lester Carter went walking along the railroad tracks?

"Price: No sir, we never have been on the railroad together.

"Leibowitz: Isn't it a fact, Mrs. Price, that you had intercourse with your boyfriend on the ground while Ruby had intercourse with Lester Carter right beside you?

"Price: We absolutely did not.

"Leibowitz: You're a pretty good little actress aren't you?"

…

"Leibowitz: Isn't the reason why you are making these charges you were found hoboing on a freight train?

"Price: I was seeking work for my mother.

"Leibowitz: And you saw the Negroes had been captured by the people at Paint Rock and you thought you would be arrested for vagrancy for being a hobo on a train in company with Negroes and at that time you determined to say they raped you to save yourself?!

"Price: No sir, I didn't!"

What Leibowitz, a Romanian immigrant who had come to New York decades earlier, had no way of realizing was that a Northern man publicly attacking the word of a Southern woman, no matter how low her status in society, stirred harsh memories for those in his audience, many of whom had been shaped by a childhood during the dreadful days of Reconstruction. As historian Mills Thornton put it, "While blacks felt that they were oppressed by Southern whites, Southern whites had a strong sense of their own oppression. They were junior partners in the American experiment, that they were not fully accepted as citizens of the United States. And they resented that." Thus, without realizing it, Leibowitz was not just fighting for the lives of his clients but also against generations of anger that went back to the Civil War.

Still, Leibowitz plugged on, next calling Dr. R.R. Bridges to the stand and questioning him about how the women looked when he examined them a few hours after the supposed rape. The doctor's testimony was damning for Price, especially when he said that the sperm he found in her was no longer motile. That would be indicative of sexual intercourse having occurred much earlier than the time of the rape just hours earlier.

A picture of Bridges testifying

Ultimately, it was Lester Carter who the attorney called to tie his case together. Carter willingly testified that he was the one who had been with Price the night before the alleged rape:

"Carter: Victoria Price said she knew where we could go and see fun, take a walk for instance.

"Leibowitz; Go ahead, what happened?

"Carter: We walked up the yards 'til we came to the (hobo) jungles.

"Leibowitz: What occurred in the hobo jungles that night?

"Carter: We all sat down near a bendin' lake of water where they was honeysuckles and a little ditch. I hung my hat on a little limb and went to having intercourse with Ruby... by firelight I saw Victoria's boyfriend had intercourse with her. ... This is what happened. It wasn't that they were raped. Victoria Price, Ruby Bates and their two boyfriends had sex. And that's all it amounts to."

After Carter's testimony, Leibowitz called each of the defendants who were not on trial that day to the stand, and each denied raping Price or Bates. Finally, he called Patterson to the stand.

"Leibowitz: Haywood Patterson: Did you have anything to do with a white girl?

"Patterson: I didn't see any girls on the train

"Leibowitz: You are a colored boy, would you dare rape a white girl

"Patterson: No sir.

"Leibowitz: Haywood Patterson, did you rape this girl?

"Patterson: No sir!"

During cross-examination, Knight tried to insinuate that Patterson was coached to deny the allegations:

Knight: "You were tried at Scottsboro?"

Patterson: "I was framed at Scottsboro."

Knight: "Who told you to say that?"

Patterson: "I told myself to say it."

The trial was almost over, but the most shocking witness was yet to come. When everyone in the courtroom thought he was about to rest his case, Leibowitz said he had one more witness. The crowd turned as the courtroom doors opened and an audible gasp was heard when Ruby Bates walked through the door. The ILD had found her and persuaded her to recant her previous testimony.

> "Leibowitz: You testified at Scottsboro that six Negroes raped you and six Negroes raped Victoria. Who coached you to say that?

> "Bates: She told it and I told it just like she told it.

> "Leibowitz: Did Victoria tell you what would happen to you if you didn't follow her story?

> "Bates: She said we might have to lay out a sentence in jail."

A picture of Bates testifying

Unfortunately for Leibowitz, he had made a tactical error, because Bates walked in dressed in obviously new and fashionable clothes and carrying a stylish purse. Knight picked up on this and pounded away on the issue, suggesting she was being paid or assisted by the defense to change her story. He was also able to produce a signed statement she had made the day after writing a letter recanting her story. The statement, made and notarized on January 6, 1932, said, "I Ruby Bates, of my own free will and accord and without any threats, promises or inducements of any kind made against or to me by any person whatever hereby make the following statements: That my evidence against the negroes at Scottsboro was absolutely the truth. That if I wrote a letter to Earl Streetman, or any other person, contradicting this testimony, on Tuesday night, January 5th, 1932 or at any other time it was when I was so drunk that I did not know what I was doing. I was drunk last night and have no recollection of writing any letter. That the letter supposed to have written by me to Streetman contains all falsehoods, no truth being in it, and I deny making any such statements or writing any such letter."

Later, in his summation for the prosecution, Morgan County Solicitor Wade Wright hammered away at the idea that Ruby Bates' testimony had been bought, and he threw in some overtly racist and sectional undertones to drive his point home: "Show them, show them that Alabama justice cannot be bought and sold with Jew money from New York. It was Brodsky, too, who brought in Ruby Bates. The same Brodsky who put the fancy city clothes, New York clothes, on Lester Carter, and I tell you, gentlemen, Ruby Bates was guilty of perjury right here in this court room. And there is such a thing as subornation of perjury…. She couldn't tell you all the things that happened in New York because part of it was in the Jew language."

Not surprisingly, Leibowitz was furious. His son later said, "He objected. He wanted, called for a mistrial immediately. Of course it was overruled." Instead, the senior Leibowitz made his own accusations: "Let us assume that the prosecution is prejudiced. Let us assume the defense is also prejudiced. Let us assume both sides are trying to prove their points. Now, I'm not going to assault your ears with any such ranting and raising the roof as you have been forced to hear from the gentleman seated over there. I shall appeal to your reason as logical, intelligent human beings, determined to give even this poor scrap of colored humanity a fair, square deal. … [Wright's words were] an appeal to prejudice, to sectionalism, to bigotry. What he is saying is, 'come on boys! We can lick this Jew from New York! Stick it into him! We're among our home folk.' … Now, I'm not getting any fee in this case and I'm not getting a penny of expenses for myself and my wife, who was here with me... I'm interested solely in seeing that that poor moronic colored boy over there and his co-defendants in the other cases get a square shake of the dice, because I believe, before God, they are the victims of a dastardly frame-up. Mobs mean nothing to me. Let them take me out and hang me. My mission will have been served if I get these unfortunates the same justice that I would seek to achieve for any of you gentlemen if you came to New York and were unjustly accused. … [Price's testimony] is the foul, contemptible lie of an abandoned, brazen woman."

After that, Knight had some final words on behalf of the prosecution, assuring the jury, "I do not want a verdict based on racial prejudice or a religious creed. I want a verdict based on the merits of this case. On that evidence, gentlemen, there can be but one verdict, and that verdict is death -- death in the electric chair for raping Victoria Price.... If you acquit this Negro, put a garland of roses around his neck, give him a supper and send him to New York City. There let Dr. Harry Fosdick dress him up in a high hat and morning coat, gray striped trousers and spats.... The State of Alabama has not framed that Negro...I don't have to have people come down here and tell me the right thing to do. I'd *nolle prosse* the indictments if I thought these Negroes were innocent. This is no framed prosecution. It is a framed defense."

Chapter 5: Carry the Great Struggle On

"Mother dear, I hope that you will get to see all my dear good friends those of whom has been sure faithful to me, although I never heard from my friends on a certain account but yet, they should know that does not discourage me as I know they carry the great struggle on and there will be no end to that until I am freed. Yes, there are at least two or three friends who are not members of the I.L.D. that I hear from. Tell William Patterson and also my many good friends that I am being held incommunicado. ... Just today I received one dollar from 80 E. 11th St., but received no letter with it that is the way it has been ever since I am here. I realize that you all know all about it and that it is why it does not worry me or discourage me therefore, it is necessary for you all not to feel discouraged anyway I am innocent of this mess and I will die with that word regardless to what may come or happen. I am innocent and I will always say I am innocent so you all need not worry as I don't worry." - Letter from Haywood Patterson to his mother, May 4, 1934

When the lawyers had finally finished, it remained for Judge Horton to instruct the jury and leave the case in its hands. He reminded the members, "[Ruby Bates] admitted on the witness stand in this trial that she had perjured herself in the other case. In considering the evidence, you may consider not only her lack of virtue as admitted by her here, but also that she contradicted her previous testimony as perjured. Regarding Victoria Price, there has been evidence here that she also was a woman of easy virtue. There has been evidence tending to show that she gave false testimony about her movements and activities in Chattanooga. That evidence has not, except by her, been denied. If in your minds the conviction of this defendant depends on the testimony of Victoria Price and you are convinced she has not sworn truly about any material point, you could not convict this defendant.... Take the evidence, sift it out and find the truths and untruths and render your verdict. It will not be easy to keep your minds solely on the evidence. Much prejudice has crept into it. It has come not only from far away, but from here at home as well. I have done what I thought to be right as the judge of this court no matter what the personal cost to me might be..."

The jury got the case at 1:00 p.m. on Saturday afternoon, and the next morning, when most of the good townspeople of Decatur were getting dresses for church, they returned the verdict, finding Patterson guilty. Judge Horton thanked them for their efforts and then announced the sentence: death in the electric chair.

While it seemed Patterson was not even shocked by the outcome, Leibowitz was devastated. He likened the verdict to "spitting on the tomb of Abraham Lincoln," and once back in New York, he bitterly complained about the jury: "If you ever saw those creatures those bigots whose mouths are slits in their faces, whose eyes popped out at you like frogs, whose chins dripped tobacco juice, bewhiskered and filthy, you would not ask how they could do it."

Undeterred, Leibowitz also started going to Harlem to participate in the Scottsboro rallies being held there and promising to continue the fight to exonerate the boys. On April 14, 1933, the *New York Times* reported, "Stirred to a frenzy by the eloquence of Samuel S. Leibowitz, who promised he would not give up his legal battle in defense of the nine Negroes in the Scottsboro case even if he had to 'sell his house and home,' a congregation of more than 4,000 persons hailed the lawyer as 'our leader' and 'a new Moses' yesterday afternoon at a meeting in the Salem Methodist Episcopal Church, 129th street and Seventh Avenue. Many of those at the meeting, which was held under the auspices of the Interdenominational Colored Ministers Alliance of New York, almost carried Mr. Leibowitz from the church pulpit at the conclusion of his speech. Hundreds crowded around him to shake his hands as he made his way down the aisle and out to a waiting automobile. Mr. Leibowitz reviewed the testimony and other aspects of the recent trial of Haywood Patterson, one of the nine defendants, whose mother was at the meeting. 'I promise you citizens of Harlem,' he said, 'that I will fight with every drop of blood in my body and with the help of God that those Scottsboro boys shall be free.' The Rev. Frederick A. Cullen, father of Countee Cullen, the Negro poet, and Pastor of the church, announced last night that $250 had been collected at the meeting as a contribution to the $25,000 being raised to fight the case."

Leibowitz was as good as his word; he quickly filed a motion with Horton to overturn the verdict. Then, much to everyone's surprise, Horton granted the motion, overturning the verdict the jury had come to and ordering a new trial. On June 22, 1993, he wrote of his concerns with inconsistencies in the evidence: "This is the State's evidence. It corroborates Victoria Price slightly, if at all, and her evidence is so contradictory to the evidence of the doctors who examined her that it has been impossible for the Court to reconcile their evidence with hers. ... The time and place and stage of this alleged act are such to make one wonder and question did such occur under such circumstances. The day is a sunshiny day the latter part in March; the time of day is shortly after the noon hour. The place is upon a gondola or car without a top. This gondola, according to the evidence of Mr. Turner, the conductor, was filled to within six inches to twelve or fourteen inches of the top with chert, and according to Victoria Price up to one and one half feet or two feet of the top. The whole performance necessarily being in plain view of any one observing the train as it passed..."

Then Horton spoke of the inconsistencies and prejudices of those involved in the case, including not just Price but the entire Jim Crow system she lived in. "Her manner of testifying and demeanor on the stand militate against her. Her testimony was contradictory, often evasive, and time and again she refused to answer pertinent questions. The gravity of the offense and the importance of her testimony demanded candor and sincerity. In addition to this the proof tends strongly to show that she knowingly testified falsely in many material aspects of the case. All this requires the more careful scrutiny of her evidence. The Court has heretofore devoted itself particularly to the State's evidence; this evidence fails to corroborate Victoria Price in those physical facts; the condition of the woman raped necessarily speaking more powerfully than any witness can speak who did not view the performance itself...History, sacred and profane, and the common experience of mankind teach us that women of the character shown in this case are prone for selfish reasons to make false accusations both of rape and of insult upon the slightest provocation for ulterior purposes. These women are shown, by the great weight of the evidence, on this very day before leaving Chattanooga, to have falsely accused two negroes of insulting them, and of almost precipitating a fight between one of the white boys they were in company with and these two negroes. This tendency on the part of the women shows that they are predisposed to make false accusations upon any occasion whereby their selfish ends may be gained."

Chapter 6: What Good Did It Do

"That thing they had here on May Day what good did it do. Not any at all. I'm still locked up in the cell. Instead of the I.L.D. trying to make it better for me here in jail they are making it harder for me by trying to demand the people to do things. Listen, send me some money. Send me three dollars like I told you in my first letter." - Letter from Olen Montgomery to his mother, May 3, 1934

If politics and controversy make strange bedfellows, none were ever any stranger than those made by Scottsboro. In a time when institutionalized segregation was the norm across the land and Communism was practically illegal, marches of blacks and whites together took place around the country. Janie Patterson, Haywood's mother, spoke side-by-side with Ruby Bates about the evils faced by African Americans in the South and the entire nation.

Unfortunately, these actions only egged Alabaman officials on, and the state quickly announced that there would be yet another trial. This time, however, Judge Horton was removed from the case and replaced with Judge William Callahan, well known for being a traditional, old-school jurist. As Patterson said of Callahan, "He couldn't get us to the chair fast enough."

Indeed, Callahan showed his colors when, after the evidence against Patterson was presented to a third set of jurors, he charged them with the following instructions: "Where the woman charged to have been raped, as in this case, is a white woman, there is a very strong presumption under the law that she will not and did not yield voluntarily to intercourse with the defendant, a Negro. And this is true whatever the station in life the prosecutrix may occupy, whether she be the most despised, ignorant and abandoned woman of the community, or the spotless virgin and daughter of a prominent home of luxury and learning."

Perhaps not surprisingly, the new jury again found Haywood guilty and sentenced him to death, and before Leibowitz could catch his breath, it was time for Norris' second trial. By this time, Victoria Price had gone through enough testifying that she thoroughly warmed to her subject. During Norris' trial, she told the jury, "I don't know whether or not the first Negro that got on top of me was the one that threw me down. I wouldn't say that the one that threw me down was the first one that raped me or not. Some Negro got on top of me. These Negroes were milling all over the car; they was running up and down the side; some of them raped me and some them Ruby Bates. ... While I was being raped some of the Negroes that were not raping me were walking up the side of the car.... While that raping was going on the Negro boys were hollering out and laughing and cuttin' up, telling each other to hurry up and get through and let him get to it, and things like that. ... I am able to identify this Negro that is sitting here by his face. I wouldn't try to point all nine of them out one by one. I know that the defendant was on the gondola. I recognize him after three years. There's lots of things that have happened that will pass from your mind in three years."

Once again, Dr. Bridges also offered testimony in Norris' trial, and it did little to help the state's case. He testified, "After [Price] removed her clothes, I gave her a physical examination. I don't remember seeing any cut on the top of her head from which any blood came. I did not find any bruises on the face. I don't remember finding any puffed up lips, or swollen lips. If I had seen that, I would have noticed it. We were looking for those things. I made an examination of the face. I didn't see anything. I didn't see any blood. I was examining her for the purpose of finding marks, if possible, and I made note of everything I saw. I don't remember finding any scratch on her face. I did not examine the chest of this woman that day; I did the next day. I did examine her abdomen. There were no cuts on the chest nor any cuts on the abdomen. I examined her back. There were no cuts on the back from which blood would come; no cuts on her legs; no abrasions or skin rubbed off on the legs; no tears of the skin near the privates at all. The vagina was not torn in any way. I found a couple of scratches on the wrist of one arm, and on the forearm of the other. ... When I examined this woman, her pulse was not fast; it was in the bounds of normal. The respiration was about normal, too. A person under excitement, as a rule, especially a woman, would show rapid pulse and rapid breathing."

Ruby Bates also testified in this trial, and again she stated unequivocally that no sort of sexual intercourse had taken place on the train. However, her testimony, along with that of the doctor, was largely ignored, and Norris was found guilty and sentenced to death.

At this point, Leibowitz persuaded the court to delay the trials of the other seven men until he could have time to prepare his case, so all nine Scottsboro Boys remained in Kilby Prison while those on the outside tried to figure out how to save their lives. At the same time, the incredible stress on the defendants caused them to become increasingly unstable, and they began to fight among themselves, often attracting the attention and nightsticks of the white guards.

Against clearly daunting odds, Leibowitz fought on, assuring those involved that he was making progress: "The appeals are now being rushed to the Alabama Supreme Court. I have every confidence in the world that we shall win there. In the event that we do not we are going right on up to the United States Supreme Court in Washington." He did indeed do this, and in February 1935, the Supreme Court heard *Norris v. Alabama*, which hinged on Leibowitz's argument that the state had illegally kept African Americans from serving on the jury. Some of the most damning pieces of evidence against the state were the jury rolls themselves, which featured lengthy lists of white prospective jurors but only a few black men added, obviously recently, at the end.

The Supreme Court reversed the Alabama Supreme Court's finding that the rolls were legal, ruling that the Equal Protection Clause of the 14th Amendment mandated that blacks could not be barred from serving as jurors or it would disrupt the right of a defendant to be tried by his peers. In his majority opinion, Chief Justice Charles Evans Hughes wrote, "That showing as to the long-continued exclusion of negroes from jury service, and as to the many negroes qualified for that service, could not be met by mere generalities. If, in the presence of such testimony as defendant adduced, the mere general assertions by officials of their performance of duty were to be accepted as an adequate justification for the complete exclusion of negroes from jury service, the constitutional provision -- adopted with special reference to their protection -- would be but a vain and illusory requirement. The general attitude of the jury commissioner is shown by the following extract from his testimony: 'I do not know of any negro in Morgan County over twenty-one and under sixty-five who is generally reputed to be honest and intelligent and who is esteemed in the community for his integrity, good character and sound judgment, who is not an habitual drunkard, who isn't afflicted with a permanent disease or physical weakness which would render him unfit to discharge the duties of a juror, and who can read English, and who has never been convicted of a crime involving moral turpitude.' In the light of the testimony given by defendant's witnesses, we find it impossible to accept such a sweeping characterization of the lack of qualifications of Negroes in Morgan County. It is so sweeping, and so contrary to the evidence as to the many qualified Negroes, that it destroys the intended effect of the commissioner's testimony."

Hughes

Chapter 7: The Outside World

"I takes the advantage of this golden opportunity in addressing you these few lines while sitting here by the window in my little cell inhaling the cool breezes as they slowly pass by and listening to the sweet music as it safely sing the song of you is my sunshine. Frankly you is my sunshine of the kind deeds you have enlighten the days of my unhappy life. You have encouraged me at the time I be discouraged. You have brought sunshine into my gloomy heart at the needy times. you have been a God fairy to me of which makes you my Earthly Sunshine, (Smile) Now I must stop to write a line of informative of my present health of which is failing me very fast, though I truly hope you is well blessed with good health and is extremely enjoying life. Many - Many Thanks for the Extra $1.00 it was very kind of you to remember me at this time, and I highly appreciate your kindness. Well I am certain you is growing tired of reading such horrible writing so I'll bring this letter to a conclusion by saying I am patiently waiting a few lines of pacification of the outside world concerning yourself and your favorite hobby (etc.)"
- Letter from Andy Wright to Mrs. Hester G. Huntington, March 15, 1942

With the Supreme Court ruling in hand, Leibowitz returned again to Alabama, where people were by now well past the point of growing tired of the embarrassment and expense of trial after trial after trial. Even Grover Hall, the editor of *The Montgomery Advertiser* and once a strong supporter of the case against the Scottsboro Boys, wrote, "The Advertiser knows, all of its readers know, the whole of this sordid, sickening story. 'Scottsboro' has stigmatized Alabama throughout the civilized world. We herewith suggest and urge that the State now move for a decent, dignified compromise. Nothing can be gained by demanding the final pound of flesh. Throw this body of death away from Alabama."

The state was willing to press for a more reasonable verdict in the fourth trial against Patterson, but only if Leibowitz stepped down and a Southern attorney took his place. He and four others were still convicted, but the state dropped charges against Montgomery, Roberson, Roy Wright and Williams. Two of them had only been 13 years old at the time of the crime, and the other two were so physically impaired that it seemed unlikely they could have done anything.

Following their acquittal, perhaps because of fears that they would be lynched if they stayed in the state, sympathetic souls arranged for them to be taken to New York, where Leibowitz and his friends joyfully welcomed them. For a short while, they were the toast of the town and popular speakers at Communist functions, but as the relevance of their case began to wear off, the young men found themselves alone in a big city. The kids from the country would soon learn that they faced many of the same prejudices and opposition in New York as they had in Alabama; they had served their purpose, and their sponsors soon moved on to other causes and other friends.

Meanwhile, the other five men remained in prison in Kilby, no longer sentenced to death but instead life in prison. The Alabama Parole Board met repeatedly to review their cases but always turned down their requests to reenter society, and like their freed brethren, they too were soon forgotten.

Ironically, this might have actually turned out to be a good thing for them, because without feeling the need to defend itself from outsiders, Alabama mellowed significantly in its feelings about the case and paroled Weems in 1943. Andy Wright and Norris were released early the following year, and Powell was paroled in 1946.

Patterson, widely viewed with revile as the worst of the lot, remained in prison tormented by memories of his arrest and conviction. "I laid on the top bunk, in a way still feeling I was on a moving freight. Nothing was standing still. I was busy living from minute to minute. Everything was rumbling. I dreamed bad dreams, with freight trains, guards' faces, and courtrooms mixed up with the look of the sky at night."

Then, on a sultry summer afternoon in 1948, Patterson broke away from his shackles, if not his dreams. He explained, "We came in off the farm and checked in for dinner on July 17. I went straight to the laundry to get ready. I put the civilian suit on under my prison uniform. I didn't tell the other guys about that. We were thinning rice at that time, working in the rice field. That was about five mile from the main prison, and maybe a quarter mile from the dog warden's house. The dog warden, he had three or four colored prisoners released to him. ... Each evening when it got cool they put on a sham race to train the dogs how to get prisoners. ... I knew what time they went off on these races. I told the others that when the dogs were in the woods on a sham race, that would give us a good gift to get away. Someone would have to overtake them, tell them of a break, and bring them back. We worked until the sun was almost completely out of sight. We were somewhere on a river bottom. All in there it was high corn. The dog warden had taken off with the hounds. So I got all the boys together and said, 'Let's go.' We hit for the woods. Captain Nutley, he fired several shots. I didn't run very far down the corn, just out of sight. I told the others, 'Get going. Go fast.'"

If anything, it seems that none of those charged ever really escaped what happened during those trying times at the height of the Depression. Patterson was later convicted of killing a man in a bar fight and died in prison in Michigan less than a decade after his escape. Andy Wright was charged with rape a second time, this time of a child, but was acquitted by a New York jury. His little brother Roy joined the Army when he was old enough and served in World War II. He also got married but killed his wife and himself in a jealous rage in 1959.

Only Norris lived long enough to see his name exonerated. In 1973, after living most of his adult life in New York, he appealed to Alabama Governor George Wallace for a pardon: "My name is Clarence Norris, one of the Scottsboro Boys. I was arrested in Alabama in 1931 and sentenced to the electric chair three times. The governor commuted my sentence to life in prison. I was released on parole twice, once in 1944, and I broke my parole and went back to prison until I got out in 1946. I broke my parole again and I have been free ever since. I want to know if Alabama still wants me."

Wallace, who remains best known for being an ardent supporter of segregation and vowing "segregation now, segregation tomorrow, segregation forever" at the height of the Civil Rights Movement, surprised many people when he did indeed pardon Norris in October 1976. The state also declared him not guilty of his convictions. Norris later said, "I never thought I'd see the day that I would go back to Alabama for any reason whatsoever. And as far as I was concerned I could have skipped that, and they could have mailed the pardon to me. But plans were made for the pardons and paroles board to give me the pardon personally in the Capitol building in Montgomery. On November 29, 1976, I returned to Alabama a free man, nearly forty-six years after being taken off that freight train. There were a few hundred people waiting at the airport, and to be frank I was scared to get off the plane. I thought there might be some crazy cracker in the crowd who would take a shot at me. But Meyerson convinced me they were all well-wishers out there. I didn't believe that but when he told me security had been arranged for, I got out of the airplane. The people were pushing and shoving, the reporters were there and the TV cameras, men were shaking my hand and women were kissing on me. I was rushed to a car. It was all a blur, although I know I was answering questions and everything. I was in a daze. I'd never seen the like and I couldn't believe it was happening in Alabama. We got to the Capitol building about eleven o'clock that morning, and there was a mob there too. Everybody was smiling and telling me how happy they were that I was free. The reporters kept asking me how it felt to be free."

Of course, Norris realized that the day was about a lot more than just him: "We all packed into the pardons and paroles board's office, and Norman Ussery made a little speech of welcome. He shook my hand and gave me the pardon. The other board members congratulated me and wished me well. Lots of pictures were being taken. We left there and went directly to the Dexter Avenue Baptist Church for a press conference. The same church where Martin Luther King Jr., started the civil rights movement. The church was full with wall-to-wall people, black and white. [NAACP Director] Roy Wilkins made a speech and several others who were involved in the case. I told the reporters I was glad to be free, that I had no hard feelings against Alabama and that the past was buried as far as my concern. I said I wanted my pardon because it was due me and because of my kids, my family. I expressed my feeling that the thing I wished for more than anything in the world was for Haywood, Ozie, Andy, Roy, Olen, Eugene, Willie and Charlie to be there with me, and that they deserved the same pardon as myself."

In fact, the rest of those pardons would not come until 2013, over 80 years after the boys were tried. Alabama Governor Robert J. Bentley told those assembled, "While we could not take back what happened to the Scottsboro Boys 80 years ago, we found a way to make it right moving forward. The pardons granted to the Scottsboro Boys today are long overdue. The legislation that led to today's pardons was the result of a bipartisan, cooperative effort. I appreciate the Pardons and Parole Board for continuing our progress today and officially granting these pardons. Today, the Scottsboro Boys have finally received justice."

Online Resources

Other 20th century history titles by Charles River Editors

Other titles about Stanford White on Amazon

Bibliography

Acker, James R. (2007), Scottsboro and Its Legacy: The Cases That Challenged American Legal and Social Justice, Praeger, New York ,

Aretha, David (2008), The Trial of the Scottsboro Boys (The Civil Rights Movement), Greensboro, North Carolina: Morgan Reynolds Publishing.

Carter, Dan T. (1979), Scottsboro: A Tragedy of the American South, Louisiana State University Press, Baton Rouge.

Goodman, James (1994), Stories of Scottsboro, Vintage Books, New York.

Haskins, James (1994), The Scottsboro Boys, Henry Holt, New York.

Patterson, Haywood; Conrad, Earl (1950). Scottsboro Boy. Doubleday.

Printed in Great Britain
by Amazon